DAILY AFFIRMATIONS

A GENTLE REMINDER – YOU ARE AMAZING

And Don't You Forget It

Misty Ingram

Table of Contents

Chapter 1: Why You Are Amazing.. 6
Chapter 2: You Are Good Enough 9
Chapter 3: Believe In Yourself 12
Chapter 4: How To Be Your Own Bestfriend 14
Chapter 5: How To Have The Best Day Everyday 18
Chapter 6: The Power of Growing 1% Each Day 21
Chapter 7: How To Reinvent Yourself and Chase Your Dreams 24
Chapter 8: Happy People Choose to Exercise 27
Chapter 9: Take Ownsership of Yourself 30
Chapter 10: Enjoying The Journey 33
Chapter 11: Living In The Moment 36
Chapter 12: The Goal Is Not The Point 39
Chapter 13: Figuring Out Your Dreams 42
Chapter 14: How To Worry Less 45
Chapter 15: How To Avoid The Hidden Danger of Comparing Yourself To Others 49
Chapter 16: How To Be Inspired 51
Chapter 17: Dealing With Feelings of Overwhelm 56
Chapter 18: How To Embrace Adventure To Change Your Life 61
Chapter 19: How To Achieve True Happiness 64
Chapter 20: Be Consistent, Not Perfect 69
Chapter 21: 6 Ways To Transform Your Thinking 72
Chapter 22: 5 Smart Ways To Deal With Toxic People 76
Chapter 23: How To Stop Getting In Your Own Way 80
Chapter 24: The Things That Matter 84
Chapter 25: How To Train Yourself To Be Optimistic and Positive ... 89
Chapter 26: How Decluttering Brings You Happiness? 92
Chapter 27: Remember The Feeling of Productivity 99

Chapter 28: Affirmations For Men 102
Chapter 29: Affirmations for Women 112
Chapter 30: Stop Hitting That Snooze Button 122

Chapter 1:

Why You Are Amazing

When was the last time you told yourself that you were amazing? Was it last week, last month, last year, or maybe not even once in your life?

As humans, we always seek to gain validation from our peers. We wait to see if something that we did recently warranted praise or commendation. Either from our colleagues, our bosses, our friends, or even our families. And when we don't receive those words that we expect them to, we think that we are unworthy, or that our work just wasn't good enough. That we are lousy and under serving of praise.

With social media and the power of the internet, these feelings have been amplified. For those of us that look at the likes on our Instagram posts or stories, or the number of followers on TikTok, Facebook, or Snapchat, we allow ourselves to be subjected to the validation of external forces in order to qualify our self-worth. Whether these are strangers who don't know you at all, or whoever they might be, their approval seems to matter the most to us rather than the approval we can choose to give ourselves.

We believe that we always have to up our game in order to seek happiness. Every time we don't get the likes, we let it affect our mood for the rest of the day or even the week.

Have you ever thought of how wonderful it is if you are your best cheerleader in life? If the only validation you needed to seek was from yourself? That you were proud of the work you put out there, even if the world disagrees, because you know that you have put your heart and soul into the project and that there was nothing else you could have done better in that moment when you were producing that thing?

I am here to tell you that you are amazing because only you have the power to choose to love yourself unconditionally. You have the power to tell yourself that you are amazing. and that you have the power to look into yourself and be proud of how far you came in life. To be amazed by the things that you have done up until this point, things that other people might not have seen, acknowledged, or given credit to you for. But you can give that credit to yourself. To pat yourself on the back and say "I did a great job".

I believe that we all have this ability to look inwards. That we don't need external forces to tell us we are amazing because deep down, we already know we are.

If nobody else in the world loves you, know that I do. I love your courage, your bravery, your resilience, your heart, your soul, your commitment, and your dedication to live out your best life on this earth.

Tell yourself each and everyday that you deserve to be loved, and that you are loved.

Go through life fiercely knowing that you don't need to seek happiness, validations, and approval from others. That you have it inside you all along and that is all you need to keep going.

Chapter 2:

You Are Good Enough

It is happening all the time to everyone in this era of technology and transparent media, where everyone feels like they are doing something wrong. Everyone at some stage feels like they are missing something. Everything is alright but their always a feeling of uncertainty that what if I do something that screws it all up.

Sounds familiar? It is because we have developed a mindset where we are always at the center of everything going wrong. We always feel like we have something to do for even the smallest of mistakes and we feel like having no clue for eradicating anyone of them.

Why are you being so hard on yourself? Why are you acting up like you are not better enough? You spend most of your time and energy figuring out why you are enough.

You can't take everything personally. You might feel a little protected is knowing that you are not alone in these feelings and these circumstances.

More than often, we do something with good intentions and still end up getting not-so-good results. Here we end up thinking that we didn't give it our best and didn't try hard enough to make things better.

The reality is that we had all the resources and all the energies and intentions, but it just wasn't meant to happen at all. It wasn't meant to happen for anyone, but you only put yourself in the front row for punishment.

Stop thinking that you are a failure. One mistake is not the end of the world. One failure is not the end of the world. You need to have the confidence in yourself that you have many more chances to prove everyone wrong and above all, to prove yourself wrong.
Keep your head up where you can see above all this catastrophe and chaos. Look deep into your achievements. If you think you are the misfortune magnet, who can you credit for your success?

It was you! You and you only! You were able and talented enough to achieve whatever you have right now. You will achieve more and bigger once you quite feel like an imposter.

You are good enough just as you are. You can feel like a loser whenever you want, but you take yourself down to the track over and over again, you will eventually end up staying on that track and no one would be at fault then but you.

So, buck up, stay strong and keep fighting if there are urges of giving up, just because one thing didn't go your way.

There are a thousand paths you can take to get to the top where you can truly appreciate your efforts and be amazed by what hurdles you were able to cross!

You should be grateful and proud of yourself and everything that you are and everything that you own.

You should remember this till your last day to do everything that you can to make you realize that whatever you have right now might not be enough, but you care enough for yourself to achieve anything and fight off any adversity.

Chapter 3:

Believe in Yourself

Listen up. I want to tell you a story. This story is about a boy. A boy who became a man, despite all odds. You see, when he was a child, he didn't have a lot going for him. The smallest and weakest in his class, he had to struggle every day just to keep up with his peers. Every minute of every hour was a fight against an opponent bigger and stronger than he was - and every day he was knocked down. Beaten. Defeated. But... despite that... despite everything that was going against him... this small, weak boy had one thing that separated him from hundreds of millions of people in this world. A differentiating factor that made a difference in the matter of what makes a winner in this world of losers. You see this boy believed in himself. No matter the odds, he believed fundamentally that he had the power to overcome anything that got in his way! It didn't matter how many times he was knocked down, he got RIGHT BACK UP!

Now it wasn't easy. It hurt like hell. Every time he failed was another reminder of how far behind he was. A reminder of the nearly insurmountable gap between him and everyone else and lurking behind that reminder was the temptation, the suggestion to just give up. Throw in the towel. Surrender the win. Yet believe me when I tell you that no matter HOW tough things got, no matter HOW much he wanted to give in, a small voice in his heart keep saying... not today... just once more... I know it hurts but I can try again... Just. Once. More.

You see more than anything in this world HE KNEW that deep inside him was a greatness just WAITING to be tapped into! A power that most people would never see, but not him. It didn't matter what the world threw at him, because he'd be damned if he let his potential die alongside him. And all it took? All it required to unlock the chasm of greatness inside was a moment to realize the lies the world tried to tell him. In less than a second he recognized the light inside that would ignite a spark of success to address the ones who didn't believe that he could do it. The ones who told him to give up! Get out! Go home and roam the streets where failure meets those who weren't born to sit at the seat at the top!

Yet what they didn't know is that being born weak didn't matter any longer 'cause in his fight to succeed he became stronger. Rising up to the heights beyond, he WOULD NOT GIVE UP till he forged a bond within his heart that ensured NO MATTER THE ODDS, no matter what anyone said about him, no matter what the world told him, he had something that NO ONE could take away from him. A power so strong it transformed this boy into a man. A loser into a winner. A failure into a success. That, is the power of self-belief...

Chapter 4:

How To Be Your Own Best Friend

Why would you want to become your own best friend? There are several benefits to creating your internal support system rather than relying on your partner, friends, or family to be there for you when you're suffering. Having other people's expectations can lead to disappointment, heartbreak, and relationship breakdown if your expectations aren't met. We all have it in us to give ourselves what we need without seeking it externally.

Of course, it's great if you have a strong support network, but you could still benefit from becoming more self-reliant. And what about if you have no one to turn to for help, or if your current support people are unable to be there for you? Isn't it far better to know how to support yourself in times of need?

Here's how to become your own best friend.

1. Be Nice To Yourself

The first step to becoming a friend is to treat yourself like you would treat a friend. That means that you need to stop being self-critical and beating yourself up. Start by acknowledging your good qualities, talents, and abilities and begin to appreciate your unique self.

When you catch yourself thinking up some nasty self-talk, stop and ask, "Would I say this to my best friend?" If not, then reframe your self-talk to be more supportive and caring.

2. Imagine How You Would Support A Friend In The Same Situation

Think about a loved one, a friend, a family member, someone dear to you and imagine that they are in the same situation you are currently facing. Think about how they're struggling, suffering, and feeling stuck with this problem, then consider how to best offer assistance and advice to them.

Craft the words that you would say to your greatest friend and then say them gently to yourself. Allow yourself to feel supported, and give yourself what you need.

3. Honor Your Needs

Following the theme of considering how you would help a dear friend, you need to start taking your advice and putting your own needs first. Do you need a day off from work? A long hot bath? An early night? A wild night? Some time to catch up on your reading, cleaning, gardening, creative projects, social life, or self-care?

Whatever you need, allow yourself to put it at the top of the list rather than the bottom. Be there for yourself and make it happen.

4. Send Compassion To The Part of You That is Hurting

Being a friend to yourself involves adopting and mastering the art of self-compassion. Compassion isn't forceful or solution focused. Compassion is accepting, peaceful, and loving, without the need to control or change anything.

Imagine a mother holding a child who has bumped his head. Her compassion is a strong force. She simply holds her child with loving, comforting, gentle arms and whispers, "It will be alright, my love." The child trusts his mother's words just as you learn to trust your own words when speaking to yourself.

Imagine yourself as both the child and the mother simultaneously. Offer compassion at the same time as you open up to receive it.

Use these techniques to become your own best friend and start being there for yourself!

Chapter 5:

How To Have The Best Day Everyday

We all have the power to create the kind of day we want to experience every time we go to sleep and wake up the next day.

It is normal to think that we will only have an amazing day when something good happens to us. We believe that good things only happen out of luck, chance, fate, or whatever, but we never think that we can create a good day just by our sheer desire to.

What the best day means to each of us may be different, some prioritize professional accomplishments as their measurement of a great day, some prioritize spending time with as many friends as possibly in a 24 hour period as one that is great. But when we depend on these circumstances, we are never really in full control of our day because bad things can always happen without a rhyme or reason. Our presentation that we have been working months on could suddenly be marred by a technical difficulty, or our friends could cancel on us last minute due to whatever reason.

What we thought would be our best day could turn out to be one filled with disappointments and maybe even loneliness.

I struggle with this all the time. Everytime, I had built up the perfect day in my head, something always seem to go wrong somehow and I am left searching for a filler to cover that void. Through the fault of nobody but life getting the way, as it always does, I found out that if I always depended on others to give me the best day, that it rarely ever happens. Occasionally things work out great when I least expect it, but those occurrences are still out of my control.

It is only when we decide for ourselves that we can have the best day regardless of life inserting itself in, that we can truly enjoy every waking moment of our lives. By constantly reminding ourselves that we are grateful to be alive, to live each moment in the present, and to live as though tomorrow might never come, we can truly appreciate the little things in life that we often overlook. We have the best day because we believe that it is.

From the moment that we get out of bed, we appreciate the first breath we take, the first shower that we take, the first meal that we take, and all the little things that make up our wonderful day. Appreciating the fact that we are living with a roof over our heads, that we have clean water to drink, air conditioning to keep us cool, heaters to keep us warm, literally anything and everything around us, there is something to be grateful for.

When we start to notice that our life is truly amazing, we will never have to depend on other things or other people to make us have our best day. That is the kind of control we have over our day if we set it off on the right foot from the get-go.

It was only when I started being grateful for the fact that I am truly blessed with an amazing family, pet, friends, a house, that I realized i didn't need fancy party or fancy things to allow me to have the best day ever. Yes, there are moments in life when we feel truly alive, those moments we will cherish and remember, but those moments are also few and far between. If we can take control of the other 364 days of the year, we would truly be the happiest people alive on this earth who are living their best days everyday.

Chapter 6:

The Power of Growing 1% Each Day

We all chase growth, we all chase success, but many of us want to be the best overnight, we want to get better 1000% over a month. We expect to lose 50 pounds by the end of the month, so we push ourselves so hard, so fast, so intensely, that we often burn out before the month has even ended.

We apply this same speed to our relationships, our careers, other aspects of our health, and we soon wonder why we cannot sustain this momentum for long.

The reason is that changes must be made gradually. Sure we can go cold turkey by cutting carbs out completely from our diet, but how many of you will agree that by the 4th day, many of us will start bingeing on that big plate of pasta because we just miss it so much.

If instead, we had cut our portions of pasta quota for the week by say 30%, how many of you would agree that it would have been a much better route to take instead of the former?

Today I want to challenge you to totally reframe how you approach change. After you have identified the areas in your life you know you need to work on, I want you to start working on one aspect at a time.

Instead of aiming for a 100% growth and transformation by the end of next week, I want you to tell yourself that you will be a 1% better version of yourself each and every day.

This mindset immediately alleviates any pressure we have on ourselves for drastic changes. Changes that are unsustainable even in the short run. By making incremental changes, we give ourselves the space to grow, to learn, to get better, and to be better.

Take your favourite sport for example. For me it's tennis. I don't expect to become like Federer overnight no matter how hard I believe I can. Instead, i break down each aspect of federer's game and work on fine adjustments to my own game 1% at a time. These 1% gains will compound over time. As with everything else that you do.

If career is an area of focus for you, instead of expecting to become employee of the month by the next month, work instead on becoming a 1% better employee each day. By the end of 100 days, you would've already become more than 100% than you were at the start of your job, and by the end of the year, you would already be so amazing at it that you would've believe how you got there in the first place.

Life is a marathon, not a sprint. If we sprint through life, we will miss all the amazing sights along the way. We will miss the fine details that make the journey worth taking. Similarly, our personal development and growth is also a marathon, not a sprint. We should all keep that in perspective when we approach any new project or endeavour. Only then can we truly make a lasting difference in the areas of our lives that matters to us most.

Chapter 7:

How To Reinvent Yourself And Chase Your Dreams

Tom Clancy was one of the most successful authors of his generation. Focusing primarily on military storylines, Clancy wrote 17 novels that became #1 New York Times best-sellers. In total, his books sold more than 100 million copies. But even with all of those amazing achievements, what I found most amazing about Clancy was his willingness to reinvent himself.

We all have goals that we say are important to us — getting in shape, building a business, writing a book, and so on — but the inertia of life holds us back for most of us. This is especially true when we're living a relatively comfortable life. Most people in Tom Clancy's situation would probably continue their insurance career rather than chase the dream of becoming a novelist.

It's easy to look at someone with the success of Tom Clancy and claim that he was destined for success. One hundred million copies sold? He must have been born to be a writer. But if you were to look at him at any point during the first 20 years of his career, you wouldn't have seen a writer at all.

And that raises an interesting question...
What made the biggest difference in Clancy's life? Was it his level of talent? Or was it his willingness to make choices and take action?
There are plenty of talented people who never choose to do something different, reinvent themselves, and pursue their dreams. It's hard to work up the guts to try something new. Nobody wants to feel stupid and start from the beginning all over again.

But talent isn't worth a thing without the willingness to take action. It's great to have a dream, but it's better to pursue it.

Tom Clancy's Advice For Writing (And Life)

"You learn to write the same way you learn to play golf. You do it and keep doing it until you get it right. Many people think something mystical happens to you. That may be the muse who kisses you on the ear. But writing isn't divinely inspired — it's hard work."
—Tom Clancy

There's nothing special that happens to the people who choose to reinvent themselves and chase their dreams. It's not any easier for them than it is for you. It's just that at some point, they choose to do the work. They choose to take action. And they choose themselves.

Reinventing yourself and developing a new skill is hard work. Going from out of shape to the best shape of your life is hard work. Transitioning from corporate desk jockey to proud entrepreneur is hard work. Moving from a life-long insurance salesman to a best-selling novelist is hard work. And so is pretty much every other goal worth fighting for.

As Clancy says, there's nothing "mystical" about it. You won't feel "divinely inspired." The first steps toward any dream are slow, unsexy, and inconvenient — sort of like writing a novel on the weekends while you're still running a small insurance agency.

And to further complicate things, reinventing yourself is particularly hard because nobody will praise you for it — especially in the beginning. Tom Clancy's wife told him to "go back to selling insurance."

The good news is that the path to doing work you love might not look the way you expected, but it can still get you to where you want to go — if you choose to try something new.

It's never too late to reinvent yourself.

Chapter 8:

Happy People Choose to Exercise

There is a feeling you get when you just finish your workout, and you feel amazing, much better than you were feeling before. Even when you are not feeling motivated to go to the gym, just thinking about this feeling makes you get up, leave your bed and get going to the gym. This feeling can also be called an endorphin rush. Exercise indeed makes you happier in multiple ways.

Firstly, movement helps you bond with others that are in the brain chemistry of it all. Your heart rate is going up, you are using your body, engaging your muscles, your brain chemistry will change, and it will make it easier for you to connect and bond with other people. It also changes how your trust people. Research also showed that social pressures like a hug, laughing, or high-five are also enhanced. You will also find your new fitness fam, the people you will be working out with, and because you will have a shared interest that is having a healthy lifestyle will help you have a stronger bond with them. And as experts say that having strong relationships and connections in life will help you in overall happiness.

We have already discussed those exercise increases endorphins but what you do not know is that it increases a lot more brain chemicals that make you feel happy and good about yourself. Some of the brain chemicals that increase are; dopamine, endorphins, endocannabinoid and adrenaline. All of these chemicals are associated with feeling confident, capable, and happy. The amount of stress, physical pain, and anxiety also decrease significantly. A chemical that your body creates when your muscles contract is called "myokine", it is also shown to boost happiness and relieve stress.

Secondly, exercise can help boost your confidence, and of course, when it comes to feeling empowered and happy, confidence is the key. "At the point when you move with others, it's anything but a solid feeling of 'greater than self' probability that causes individuals to feel more idealistic and enabled, "Also, it permits individuals to feel more engaged turning around the difficulties in their own lives. What's more, that is a fascinating side advantage of moving with others because there's an encapsulated feeling of 'we're in the same boat' that converts into self-assurance and the capacity to take on difficulties in your day; to day existence."

Thirdly, exercising outdoors affects your brain, similar to meditation. In case you're similar to the innumerable other people who have found out about the advantages of contemplation yet can't make the time, uplifting news. You may not need to contemplate to get a portion of the advantages. Researchers found that exercising outside can similarly affect the cerebrum and disposition as reflection. Exercising outside immediately affects a state of mind that is amazingly incredible for wretchedness and nervousness. Since it's anything but a state in your mind that is the same as contemplation, the condition of open mindfulness,"

Chapter 9:

Take Ownership of Yourself

What belongs to you but is used by other people more than you?

Your name.

And that's okay. People can use your name. But you must never allow yourself to lose ownership of you. In fact, you need to be incredibly conscious of taking ownership of everything that you are. And I do mean everything. Those few extra pounds, the nose you think is too big, your ginger hair or freckled skin. Whatever it is that you are insecure about, it's time that you showed up and took ownership. Because the moment you do your world will change.

But what does that look like? Why does it matter?

If someone parks a limo in the road outside your house, hands you the keys and tells you it is yours, what would you do? You're not just gonna put the keys in the ignition and leave it in the road. You are going to put that thing in a garage and get it insured. You will make sure that it is in a place where it is safe from weather and your jealous neighbour. Those are the things that you do when you take ownership of something. You make sure that they are protected because you value them. Then when you drive around town you don't look around as if you've stolen the thing. You drive with style and confidence. You are bold and comfortable because it belongs to you. That is what ownership looks like.

Now I know what you're thinking. That's easy to do with a limo, but I what I have is the equivalent of a car built before World War two. But the beautiful thing about ownership is that it does not depend on the object. It is not the thing being owned that you have to worry about, all you have to do is claim it. You've seen teenagers when they get their first car. Even if it is an old rust-bucket they drive around beaming with pride. Why? Because they know that what they have is theirs. It belongs to them and so they take ownership of it.

You have to do the same. You must take ownership of every part of you because in doing so you will keep it secure. You no longer have to be insecure about your weight if you know that that is where you are at right now. That doesn't mean you don't work for change though. It doesn't give you an excuse for stagnancy. You take accountability for your change and growth as much as you do for your present state. But in taking ownership you work towards polishing your pride, not getting rid of your low self-esteem. The difference may sound semantic, but the implications are enormous. The one allows you to work towards something and get somewhere good. The other makes it feel like you are just running away from something. And when you are running away then the only direction that matters is away – even if that means you run in circles.

Make a change today. Own yourself once more and be amazed at the rush that comes with it. With ownership comes confidence.

Chapter 10:

Enjoying The Journey

Today I want to talk about why enjoying the journey of life is important. And why hurrying to get to the destination might not be all that enjoyable as we think it is.

A lot of us plan our lives around an end goal, whether it be getting to a particular position in our company's ladder, or becoming the best player in a sport, or having the most followers on Instagram or whatever the goal may be... Many of us just can't wait to get there. However, many a times, once we reach our goal, whilst we may feel a sense of satisfaction and accomplishment for a brief moment, we inevitably feel like something is missing again and we search for our next objective and target to hit.

I have come to realize that in life, it is not always so much the end goal, but the journey, trials, struggles, and tribulations that make the journey there worth it. If we only focus on the end goal, we may miss out the amazing sights along the way. We will ultimately miss the point of the journey and why we embarked on it in the first place.

Athletes who achieve one major title never stop at just that one, they look for the next milestone they can achieve, but they enjoy the process, they take it one step at a time and at the end of their careers they can look back with joy that they had left no stone unturned. And that they can live their life without regret.

How many times have you seen celebrities winning the biggest prize in their careers, whether it may be the Grammy's Album of the Year if you are a musician, or the Oscars Best Actor or Best Actress Award? How many of them actually feel like that is the end of the journey? They keep creating and keep making movies and film not because they want that award, even though it is certainly a nice distinction to have, but more so because they enjoy their craft and they enjoy the art of producing.

If winning that trophy was the end goal, we would see many artists just end their careers there and then after reaching the summit. However, that is not the case. They will try to create something new for as long as people are engaged with their craft, as with the case of Meryl Streep, even at 70+ she is still working her butt off even after she has achieved all the fame and money in the world

Even for myself, at times I just want to reach the end as quickly as possible. But many times, when I get there, I am never satisfied. I feel empty inside and I feel that I should be doing more. And when I rush to the end, I do feel like I missed many important sights along the way that would have made the journey much more rewarding and enjoyable had I told myself to slow it down just a little.

I believe that for all of us, the journey is much more important than the destination. It is through the journey that we grow as a person, it is through the journey that we evolve and take on new ideas, work ethics, knowledge, and many little nuggets that make the trip worth it at the end. If someone were to hand you a grand slam title without having you earned it, it would be an empty trophy with no meaning and emotions behind it. The trophy would not represent the hours of hard work that you have put in to be deserving of that title.

So, I challenge each and everyone of you today to take a step back in whatever journey you may be on. To analyze in what aspects can you enjoy the moment and to not place so much pressure into getting to the destination asap. Take it one day at a time and see how the journey you are on is actually a meaningful one that you should treasure each day and not let up.

Chapter 11:

Living in the Moment

Today we're going to talk about a topic that will help those of you struggling with fears and anxieties about your past and even about your future. And I hope that at the end of this video, you may be able to live a life that is truly more present and full.

So, what is living in the moment all about and why should we even bother?

You see, for many of us, since we're young, we've been told to plan for our future. And we always feel like we're never enough until we achieve the next best grade in class, get into a great university, get a high paying career, and then retire comfortably. We always look at our life as an endless competition, and that we believe that there will always be more time to have fun and enjoy life later when we have worked our asses off and clawed our way to success. Measures that are either set by our parents, society, or our peers. And this constant desire to look ahead, while is a good motivator if done in moderation and not obsessively, can lead us to always being unhappy in our current present moment.

Because we are always chasing something bigger, the goal post keeps moving farther and farther away every time we reach one. And the reality is that we will never ever be happy with ourselves at any point if that becomes our motto. We try to look so far ahead all the time that we miss the beautiful sights along the way. We miss the whole point of our goals which is not to want the end goal so eagerly, but to actually enjoy the process, enjoy the journey, and enjoy each step along the way. The struggles, the sadness, the accomplishments, the joy. When we stop checking out the flowers around us, and when we stop looking around the beautiful sights, the destination becomes less amazing.

Reminding ourselves to live in the present helps us keep things in perspective that yes, even though our ultimate dream is to be this and that career wise, or whatever it may be, that we must not forget that life is precious, and that each day is a blessing and that we should cherish each living day as if it were your last.

Forget the idea that you might have 30 years to work before you can tell ur self that you can finally relax and retire. Because you never know if you will even have tomorrow. If you are always reminded that life is fragile and that your life isn't always guaranteed, that you become more aware that you need to live in the moment in order to live your best life. Rid yourself of any worries, anxieties, and fears you have about the future because the time will come when it comes. Things will happen for you eventually so long as you do what you need to do each and every day without obsessing over it.

Sometimes our past failures and shortcomings in the workplace can have an adverse effect on how we view the present as well. And this cycle perpetuates itself over and over again and we lose sight of what's really important to us. Our family, our friends, our pets, and we neglect them or neglect to spend enough time with them thinking we have so much time left. But we fail to remember again that life does not always work the way we want it to. And we need to be careful not to fall into that trap that we have complete and total control over our life and how our plans would work out.

In the next video we will talk about how to live in the moment if you have anxieties and fears about things unrelated to work. Whether it be a family issue or a health issue. I want to address that in a separate topic.

Chapter 12:

The Goal Is Not The Point

If you ever want to achieve your goals, stop thinking about them. I know this goes against everything anyone has ever said about achieving your goals.

Everyone says that think about one thing and then stick to it. Devote yourself to that one single goal as you are committed to your next breath. Check on your goals over and over again to see if you are still on track or not and you will get there sooner than you think.

What I am proposing is against all the theories that exist behind achieving your goals but wait a minute and listen to me.

The reason behind this opposing theory is that we spend more time concentrating on thinking and panning about our goals. Rather than actually doing something to achieve them.

We think about getting into college. Getting a Bachelor's degree and then getting our Master's degree and so on. So that we can finally decide to appear for an interview that we have dreamed about or to start a business that we are crazy about.

But these are not the requirements for any of them to happen. You can get a degree in whatever discipline you want or not, and can still opt for business. As far as job interviews are concerned, they are not looking for the most educated person for that post. But the most talented and experienced person that suits the role on hand.

So we purposefully spend our life doing things that carry the least importance in actual to that goal.

What we should be doing is to get started with the simplest things and pile upon them as soon as possible. Because life is too short to keep thinking.

Thinking is the easiest way out of our miseries. Staying idol and fantasizing about things coming to reality is the lamest thing to do when you can actually go out and start discovering the opportunities that lie ahead of you.

Your goals are things that are out of your control. You might get them, you might not. But the actions, motivation, and the effort you put behind your goal make the goal a small thing when you actually grab it. Because then you look back and you feel proud of yourself for what you have achieved throughout the journey.

At the end of that journey, you feel happier and content with what you gained within yourself irrespective of the goal. Because you made yourself realize your true potential and your true purpose as an active human being.

Find purpose in the journey for you can't know for sure about what lies ahead. But what you do know is that you can do what you want to do to your own limits. When you come to realize your true potential, the original goal seems to fade away in the background. Because then your effort starts to appear in the foreground.

A goal isn't always meant to be achieved as it might not be good for you in the end or in some other circumstances. But the efforts behind these goals serve as something to look back on and be amazed at.

Chapter 13:

Figuring Out Your Dreams

Today we're going to talk about dreams and why it is important that we all have some form of a dream or aspiration that we can work towards.

For many of us who are educated in the traditional school system, we process from one grade to the next without much thought and planning besides getting into a good school. And this autopilot has caused many kids, including myself, to not have a vision of my future and what I would like to become when I grow up. We are all taught in some shape or form that we would need to choose a career and pursue that path. Dedicating years of higher education and hundreds of hours of curriculum work only to find ourselves hating the course that we had spent all this time and energy undertaking when we step into our jobs.

This has caused many to start doubting and questioning what we ought to really do with our lives and we might get really anxious because this was certainly not part of the plan that we had set out since we were young.

What I have found personally is that I spent the time and effort to pursue a higher education not because I really wanted To, but rather to appease my parents that they did not waste all their time and money on producing me with proper schooling.

I did not however, go into my field of practice that I had spent the prior 3 years studying for. Instead upon graduating, that was when I really started to figure out what I really wanted to do with my life. Luckily for my parents, they were willing to give me the time and space to explore different possible passions and to carve out a path on my own.

I realized that as I started exploring more, and learning more about myself, the dream that I thought i once had started to change. Instead of dreaming of the perfect job and having the perfect boss, I now dreamt of freedom. To achieve freedom of time to pursue my passions, and to take steps that would move me one step closer to that dream as soon as possible.

Why this particular dream you ask? As i started exploring on successful people who have made it big in life, I realized that those that were truly happy with what they were doing, were not doing things for the money, but rather that they were able to quit their full-time jobs to pursue their interests because somehow they had found a way to achieve time freedom that is irrespective of money. It amazed me how many found success by having the freedom to work from home, to not be bound by a desk job or to be hounded on my their bosses. Some live for the climb up the corporate ladder, but i knew that wasn't going to work for me. And I knew i had to make something else work to survive.

So, I decided to dedicate my time and energy to only doing things that would help me achieve freedom and that became my dream to retire early and live off my past works.

The takeaway for today is that I want you to give yourself the chance to explore different things and take a step back to assess whether your current dream will actually serve you well in the long run, or if u don't even have a dream, whether you need to take time off to go find that dream for yourself.

I challenge each and everyone of you today to keep an open mind that dreams can change, and you can always pursue a new path should you choose to. Because as the saying goes, the only constant in life is change.

Chapter 14:

How To Worry Less

How many of you worry about little things that affect the way you go about your day? That when you're out with your friends having a good time or just carrying out your daily activities, when out of nowhere a sudden burst of sadness enters your heart and mind and immediately you start to think about the worries and troubles you are facing. It is like you're fighting to stay positive and just enjoy your day but your mind just won't let you. It becomes a tug of war or a battle to see who wins?

How many of you also lose sleep because your mind starts racing at bedtime and you're flooded with sad feelings of uncertainty, despair, worthlessness or other negative emotions that when you wake up, that feeling of dread immediately overwhelms you and you just feel like life is too difficult and you just don't want to get out of bed.

Well, If you have felt those things or are feeling those things right now, I want to tell you you're not alone. Because I too struggle with those feelings or emotions on a regular basis.

At the time of writing this, I was faced with many uncertainties in life. My business had just ran into some problems, my stocks weren't doing well, I had lost money, my bank account was telling me I wasn't good enough, but most importantly, I had lost confidence. I had lost the ability to face each day with confidence that things will get better. I felt that i was worthless and that bad things will always happen to me. I kept seeing the negative side of things and it took a great deal of emotional toll on me. It wasn't like I chose to think and feel these things, but they just came into my mind whenever they liked. It was like a parasite feeding off my negative energy and thriving on it and weakening me at the same time.

Now your struggles may be different. You may have a totally different set of circumstances and struggles that you're facing, but the underlying issue is the same. We all go through times of despair, worry, frustration, and uncertainty. And it's totally normal and we shouldn't feel ashamed of it but to accept that it is a part of life and part of our reality.

But there are things we can do to minimize these worries and to shift to a healthier thought pattern that increases our ability to fight off these negative emotions.

I want to give you 5 actionable steps that you can take to worry less and be happier. And these steps are interlinked that can be carried out in fluid succession for the greatest benefit to you. But of course, you can choose whichever ones speaks the most to you and it is more important that you are able to practice any one of these steps consistently rather than doing all 5 of them haphazardly. But I want to make sure I give you all the tools so that you can make the best decisions for yourself.

Try this with me right now as I go through these 5 steps and experience the benefit for yourself instead of waiting until something bad happens.

The very first step is simple. Just breathe. When a terrible feeling of sadness rushes into your body out of nowhere, take that as a cue to close your eyes, stop whatever you are doing, and take 5 deep breaths through your nose. Breathing into your chest and diaphragm. Deep breathing has the physiological benefit of calming your nerves and releasing tension in the body and it is a quick way to block out your negative thoughts. Pause the video if you need to do practice your deep breathing before we move on.

And as you deep breathe, begin the second step. Which is to practice gratefulness. Be grateful for what you already have instead of what you think u need to have to be happy. You could be grateful for your dog, your family, your friends, and whatever means the most to you. And if you cannot think of anything to be grateful for, just be grateful that you are even alive and walking on this earth today because that is special and amazing in its own right.

Next is to practice love and kindness to yourself. You are too special and too important to be so cruel to yourself. You deserve to be loved and you owe it to yourself to be kind and forgiving. Life is tough as it is, don't make it harder. If you don't believe in yourself, I believe in you and I believe in your worthiness as a person that you have a lot left to give.

The fourth step is to Live Everyday as if it were your last. Ask yourself, will you still want to spend your time worrying about things out of your control if it was your last day on earth? Will you be able to forgive yourself if you spent 23 out of the last 24 hours of your life worrying? Or will you choose to make the most out of the day by doing things that are meaningful and to practice love to your family, friends, and yourself?

Finally, I just want you to believe in yourself and Have hope that whatever actions you are taking now will bear fruition in the future. That they will not be in vain. That at the end of the day, you have done everything to the very best of your ability and you will have no regrets and you have left no stone unturned.

How do you feel now? Do you feel that it has helped at least a little or even a lot in shaping how you view things now? That you can shift your perspective and focus on the positives instead of the worries?

If it has worked for you today, I want to challenge you to consistently practice as many of these 5 steps throughout your daily lives every single day. When you feel a deep sadness coming over you, come back to this video if you need guidance, or practice these steps if you remember them on your own.

Chapter 15:

How To Avoid The Hidden Danger of Comparing Yourself To Others

"Everybody is a genius. But if you judge a fish by its ability to climb a tree, it will live its whole life believing that it is stupid." - Albert Einstein.

Comparing yourself to others allows them to drive your behavior. We tend to compare ourselves with people over several things. It could either be something genetic, like wishing to be taller or having a deeper voice. Or something that the other person naturally does well, but we envy them since we cannot achieve their level of perfection. Sometimes the comparison can be motivating, but a lot of the time, it's destructive.

You can be anything, but you can never be everything. When we compare ourselves to others, we often compare their best features against our average ones. For example, we try to play an instrument with our left hand while being right-handed, just because Sally at work plays it well like this. The unconscious realization that we are not naturally better than them often becomes self-destructive. But we have to understand that there's only one thing we're better at than all the other people; being ourselves. This is the only game we can win.

Life is all about becoming a better version of yourself every day. The moment we start with this mindset, the world around us starts to look better again. No longer do we have to stand relative to others when our only focus and energy is placed on what we're capable of now and how to improve ourselves. By putting our effort and energy into upgrading our operating system every day, we would become happier and free from all the shackles of false comparisons. Our focus would only be on the present moment. The only person you should compare yourself to is yourself, who you were yesterday and grew into today. The way people look at you is the same way you look at people, through a distorted lens shaped by experiences and expectations. But know that you don't owe anyone anything. It would help if you only strived to work on yourself and improve yourself.

Stop comparing yourself with people and focus internally; you will start better at what matters to you. It might sound simple, but it's not easy. Play your own game instead of stealing someone else's scoreboard. Find comfort in knowing that someone will always be less than you in things you're good at. Don't steal away your happiness by comparing yourself with others. As Theodore Roosevelt once said, "Comparison is the thief of joy." You are so much more capable than you think, so don't strip off this joy from yourself. You are unique and amazing on your own!

Chapter 16:

How To Be Inspired

We all feel uninspired at times. The good news is that it's a natural part of the creative process and something everyone struggles with. The next time you're stuck in a creative dead zone, read this list of 25 things you can do to get inspired.

1. Change Your Environment

Get out of the house and go somewhere new. A new environment can spark inspiration by giving you a new way of looking at things.

2. Learn Something New

Get outside the boundaries of your own knowledge to learn something new. Learn ten words in a foreign language, research the music of 17th century Europe or pick up a star chart and learn about our universe.

3. Create A Vision Board

Think about what you want for your life and start envisioning it. Collect pictures and words that depict this life and bring them together in a vision board.

4. Get Back To Nature

Take some time out in nature and appreciate its amazing beauty. Go for a hike through the bush, climb a mountain or simply have a picnic by the pond in your local park.

5. Visit Your Local Bookstore

Bookstores are full of creative inspiration. Spend some time browsing the shelves and get inspired by the beautiful images and interesting ideas.

6. Try A New Creative Art Form

Push yourself outside the bounds of your creative specialty and try something new. If you're a writer, try painting. If you're a musician, write a poem.

7. Keep A Notebook to Jot Down Ideas

Keep a notebook with you to jot down ideas whenever they strike. These ideas might not seem ground breaking at the time but they might serve as inspiration at a later date.

8. Learn About The History Of Your Craft

Learn about how your creative craft originated, who the pioneers and greats were and how it has progressed over time. In every craft's history, there is much inspiration to be found.

9. Research What Others In Your Field Are Doing

Learn about what other people in your creative field are doing. A quick google search can be a great source of inspiration when you are low on ideas.

10. Listen To A New Type Of Music

Seek out music that is different to what you usually listen to and try it out. What about jazz, classical or rap?

11. Try Meditating

Take some time to sit, be still and breathe. Our busy lives can sometimes leave us so frantic that it can be difficult to get inspired. By taking the time out to meditate, you'll give your brain a chance to refresh.

12. Follow Ten People Who Inspire You On Twitter

We've all got creative idols. Go follow yours on twitter and get inspired every day by their musings.

13. Give Yourself The Gift Of Time

Don't rush yourself. Give yourself a day to just be and do whatever comes to you. You might be surprised at the inspiration that strikes when you least expect it.

14. Read An Inspiring Blog Post

Visit your favorite bloggers and read an inspiring post. There's nothing like a few powerful words to spark your inspiration.

15. Go Beyond Your Comfort Zone

It's easy to get stuck in a routine. Try something you've never done before that pushes you out of your comfort zone. By breaking the routine of your daily life, you'll encourage the flow of ideas and increase motivation.

Chapter 17:
Dealing With Feelings of Overwhelm

Today we're going to talk about a topic that deals with feelings of stress and overwhelm, whether it be from your job or from your family and relationships. I hope that by the end of this video that you will be able to have strategies put in place to help you better cope with the feelings and manage your emotions much better. Hopefully you will also be able to eliminate the things in your life that brings your health into question. My job here is to help you as much as I can so let's begin.

First, we have to identify the areas in your life that is bringing you unwanted stress and anxiety. I'm sure that if you think a little harder and dig a little deeper, you will be able to list out the things that are causing you to lose sleep over. The thought of that particular thing would trigger an immediate negative response in your body and only you know what they are.

So, let's begin by just brainstorming and listing them down one by one. Take as much time as you need for this exercise. Next, I want you to go through your list and arrange them according to which brings the most to the least stress. Now that you have this list, we can talk about the strategies that we can engage in to either reduce or eliminate this overwhelm.

Overwhelm can come from areas in our lives that we feel that we feel are out of control. We feel that we do not have a steady hand or the ability to manage this problem that it manifests into something that suddenly feels too big to handle. It could be something that you dread doing that you have procrastinated on, and that the problem just keeps growing bigger and bigger to the point where you don't even want to touch it. It could be from workloads being piled on top of you one after another by your bosses. It could be a project that you undertook that just maybe is too big for you to handle at your current level and expertise. It could be your family who is giving you additional problems that you have to deal with on top of your workload that is just driving you up the wall. Whatever the stresses are that contributes to your problem, know that they are valid, know that they are real and that they are normal.

Everyone goes through periods of their lives when things just all seem to happen at once. Whether it be having a new baby, a new promotion, a new career, starting a new chapter in life, it is usually those big changes in life that we face overwhelm due to the sudden and added workload that we are not used to. Overwhelm can cause us to lose sleep, lose appetite, gain weight, experience chronic stress, and all these negative aspects can surface in our bodies in ways that affect our health and wellness. When we see these triggers, it is time to make some changes.

We can start by slowing things down a little and carving out time for ourselves to be alone and to recharge. I believe great way for us to get in touch with ourselves is through yoga and meditation. While it might seem like fluff at first, I have personally tried it myself and it is in those moments of calm and relaxation that my head is truly clear. When I am actually able to hear my own thoughts and be aware of what is happening around me. During times we feel overwhelm, things can happen so fast that we lose track of who we are. And sometimes all we need to do is to bring back the attention to ourselves. Find a meditative yoga practice on audible or YouTube, or even Apple Music and Spotify if it is available. Let the teacher guide you through the practice. And just let yourself go for that 30mins or 1 hour that you choose to set aside for yourself. You will be amazed at how calm you will feel and how clear your goals will be if you do it on a regular basis.

With this clarify you may be able to make better decisions that hopefully helps you get through your rough periods that much easier. Whenever you find yourself feeling stress and overwhelm, just give yourself another 15mins to be calm and be guided through a short meditation practice.

The next thing we can do to help alleviate feelings of overwhelm is to practice slow and deep breathing. Focusing on the breath as been proven to reduce stress by triggering a physiological response in our body. We trick our brain into slowing down and focusing on one thing and one thing only. This trick can help to calm you in moments of deep anxiety when you feel the world is crashing down on you and you are not sure what to do. Just sit still for a moment and engage in this practice.

Now we have to address the elephant in the room which is what are the areas in your life that are triggering these responses from your body that is causing you to feel overwhelm. And is there any way we can eliminate these stressors from your life. Again, as I have said many times before, if this thing you are doing is bringing you such immense dread and overwhelm, maybe it is time you simply walk away from it forever if that is an option. You have to ask yourself if what you are doing can justify putting your mental and physical state in jeopardy. Whether maybe the money is worth risking your health over, or whether this person is worth keeping in your life if he or she brings you much anguish. I always believe that life is too short to be filled with things that overwhelm us. A little stress is good for us but chronic and prolonged periods of exposure to this can in fact cause us to die sooner. As cortisol is constantly being pumped into your bloodstream it can have serious negative consequences for our physical health, not to mention our mental health in the form of depression.

Sometimes we have to tell ourselves it is okay to simply walk away when we have no other option. Something or someone else will turn up that is better for us if we put ourselves first.

So, I urge all of you to take a hard look at the list you have created today. Which ones on those lists have you been suffering for prolonged periods of time with seemingly no end to it? Could you eliminate it from your life or take a smaller role on it? Always remember that you are what you take on, and that you have the power to decide what you want in your life. I believe you know how to make the right decisions for yourself as well.

Chapter 18:

How to Embrace Adventure to Change Your Life

Human beings are creatures of habit. This can be a good thing, as the habits we form can allow us to autopilot through the more tedious aspects of life. But as the years go by, many of us put not only a few habits but our entire lives on autopilot. And when we do so, we develop a problem of sameness. We stagnate, and our once-steady supply of new experiences dries up.

So, what's the cost of this?

When we stop engaging in the new, we stop developing as people. We stop growing. And when we stop growing, the monotony and boredom set in, often felt in the form of a nagging feeling that something just isn't right in our lives. If that sounds like you, it might be time to break out of the habits causing you to stagnate. To help you do this, let's look at ways you can bring adventure back into your life.

You get up. You eat a lackluster breakfast. You rush to work. You get off at 6. You watch television for a few hours. You go to bed. You repeat. Sound familiar?

Sameness has a way of making us feel like monotony is normal. We stop living, begin merely existing, and—amazingly—we feel comfortable in that. But the simple act of shaking up your routine can open your eyes to the world of adventure that's always just outside your door.

Add a Third Space

What's a third place, you might ask? In short, it's one of the keys to adventure!

A third place is somewhere that is separate from your two most-visited social environments: work and home. It's the local coffee shop where you might go to work on your latest short story. It's the barbershop where you'd go to have a chat about the latest happenings in the neighborhood. It's the library you run for when you need a quiet moment of contemplation.

Unlike someone's first place, which is the home, and the second place, which is work, the third place tends to blend community life and self-expression. It's a place where, unlike at work, you can relax and be yourself, and unlike at home, you're pushed to explore new possibilities, often through social interaction. Finding your third place, whatever that might be, is essential to breaking up the monotony of life and finding new adventures and new people. Start scouring your neighborhood for one today!

Choose a New Path

It's the experience of life that we remember the most, and it is the memories of these experiences make us happiest in old age. Regret is built upon a life of sameness—don't let that be you.

Change your habits. Change your life. Find adventure.

Now, get out there and do it.

Chapter 19:

How To Achieve True Happiness?

How many of us actually know what happiness really is? And how many of us spend our whole lives searching for it but never seem to be happy?

I want to share with you my story today of how i stumbled upon true happiness and how you can achieve the same for yourself in your life.

Many of us go through the motion of trying to earn money because we think the more money we have, the better our lives will be. We chase the dream of increasing our earning power so that we can afford to buy nicer and more expensive things. And we believe that when we have more money, our happiness level will increase as well, and we will be filled with so much money and happiness that we can finally stop chasing it.

Now I just wanna say, yes, for those who come from a not so affluent background where they have a family to feed and basic needs have to be met to in order for them to survive, having a monetary goal to work towards is truly commendable as their drive, motivation, and sole purpose comes from supporting their family. Their sense of achievement, joy, and happiness comes from seeing their loved ones attaining basic needs and then go on to achieve success later in life at the expense of their time and energy. But they are more than okay with that and they do so with a willing heart, mind, and soul. You might even say that these people have achieved true happiness. Not because they are chasing more money, but because they are using that money to serve a greater purpose other than themselves.

But what about the rest of us who seemingly have everything we could ever want but never seem to be happy? We work hard at our jobs every single day waiting for our next promotion so that we can command a higher pay. And as our income grows, so does our appetite and desire for more expensive material things.

For guys we might chase that fancy new watch like Rolex, omega, Breitling, drooling over that model that always seem to be on a never-ending waitlist. And as we purchased one, feeling that temporary joy and satisfaction, we quickly look towards that next model as the shiny object we have starts to slowly fade. We lose our so-called happiness in time and We go back to work dreaming about that next watch just to feel that joy and excitement again. This could apply to other material things such as a shiny new technology gadgets smartphone, tv, and even cars.

For women, while might not be true for everyone, they might look towards that designer shoe, that branded handbag, are that fancy jewelry that costs thousands of dollars to purchase but happily pay for it because they think it makes them feel better about ourselves. Or they could even use these purchases as retail therapy from their stressful lives and jobs.

Whatever these expensive purchases may be, we think that by spend our hard-earned money on material things, it will bring us happiness and joy, but somehow it never does, and in most cases, it is only temporary satisfactions.

That was exactly what happened with me. I kept chasing a higher income thinking it would bring me happiness. As a lover of technology, I always sought to buy the latest gadgets I could get my hands on. The excitement peaks and then fades. For me I realized that I had created an endless loop of trying to chase happiness but always coming up short.

One day I sat down and reflected on what exactly made me REALLY happy and I started writing down a list.

My List Came down to these in no particular order: Spending time with family, spending time with friends, helping others, having a purpose in life, being at peace with myself, working on my own dreams, singing and making music, exercising, being grateful, and finally being a loving person to others.

As I went through this list, I realized that hey, in none of the list did i write "making more money" or "buying more things". And it finally dawned on me that these are REALLY the things that made me truly happy. And only after I had defined these things did i actively choose to do more of them every single day.

I started spending more quality time with my friends and family, I started playing my favourite sport (Tennis) a few times a week, I chose to be grateful that I can even be alive on this earth, and I chose to be more loving and humble. Finally, I also actively chose not to compare myself to people who were more "successful" than I was because comparing yourself to others can NEVER make you happy and will only make you feel inferior when you are not. Always remember that You are special, you are unique, and you are amazing.

After doing these things every single day, I had become a much happier person. It is all about perspective.

So, what can you do to achieve happiness for yourself?

I recommend that you do the same thing I did which is to write down a list under the title "When Am I The Happiest?" or "When Was A Time When I Truly Felt Happy?" Start breaking down these memories as you recall your past, and down the essence of the memory. Everybody's list will be different as happiness means different things to every one of us. Once you have your answer, start doing more of these things everyday and tell me how you feel afterwards.

Some days you will forget about what makes you truly happy as you get bombarded by the harsh and cruel things life will throw at you. So I encourage you to put this list somewhere visible where you can see it everyday. Constantly remind yourself of what happiness means to you and shift your mind and body towards these actions every single day. I am sure you will be much happier person after that.

Chapter 20:

Be Consistent, Not Perfect

It's often drilled into our heads that we have to be **great** at everything we do. It sounds like a lot of pressure, right? Well, what if the key wasn't in being great but simply showing up all the time, over and over?
Lasting progress isn't about being consistently great; it's about being great at being consistent. That means, instead of focusing on doing things perfectly, you simply focus on just the doing and getting better as you progress. When we focus on being consistent, we give ourselves more of an opportunity for greatness.

We're constantly seeing others online who are seemingly achieving greatness overnight—leaving us feeling stuck. But what if i told you that the true power is in the process?

When we aim for consistency over perfection, these are the benefits:

1. You're Taken More Seriously By Those Around You

you can tell people until you're blue in the face what you **want** to do, but if you don't do it, they'll stop listening. However, if you show up every day and make a consistent effort, you'll be synonymous with what you're putting out there. Others will see from your actions that you're passionate about what you do or believe in.

2. You'll Make Progress

how many times have you prolonged doing something until it became practically nonexistent because you kept waiting for it to be perfect? It was a hard pill to swallow, but i found out that my fear archetype was the procrastinator a few months ago. I've always considered myself a perfectionist, and I find out procrastination is one of our key traits. We tweak things repeatedly, hoping to make them perfect, and end up never actually taking action. When we show up consistently, despite how perfect something may or may not be, we increase the possibility of progress.

By bringing more consistency into our lives, we'll have the opportunity to see true change in our circumstances. When we harp on perfection, it can often stunt our ability to grow. So, how do you become more consistent?

First, understand that you might mess up. And that's okay.
The biggest thing holding us back from being more consistent and instead relying on perfection is that we're afraid of making mistakes. When we mess up, we feel discouraged, and a way of protecting ourselves is by trying to control the outcome. So, we wait until the time is perfect instead of taking the risk.

Allow yourself the space to be brave with your life. When faced with that fear, remind yourself that it's okay to make mistakes. To help, try reciting mantras like, "I may stumble, but I'll continue to learn and get better along the way."

A Small Step Is Always Better Than No Step At All

The most beneficial thing we can do for ourselves if we ever want to see change is to take action. Whether big or small, you are putting yourself out there, and doing the work consistently adds up. When we settle into the comfort of perfection, we stifle our potential.

So today or tomorrow, take one small action that will help move you in the direction you seek. And after that, do another small thing.

Along the way, praise your small wills and honor your process. With time and a steady effort, the things you desire will begin to manifest themselves.

Chapter 21:

6 Ways to Transform Your Thinking

Changing your mindset isn't easy, but an open and positive attitude. Personal growth contributes to our choices to achieve physical, emotional, and spiritual well-being. Even something as simple as changing your mind can change your life. It's essential to take time for your mindset. During this period, we begin to understand ourselves, making us more compassionate and patient with ourselves. Our societies and cultures thrive in the professions that life brings to our lives and our tables. In this regard, the use of "bandage" solutions and rapid remedies to overcome certain obstacles in our lives have implications. These decisions never last long and are a matter of time and effort to slow down, ground up, and shift focus. Changing your mind means becoming more optimistic and giving your mind the breathing space it needs to grow and expand. It's about looking at everything that doesn't work for you and being open to other methods that might help.

1. Practice Mindfulness

To adopt a more positive mindset, you must first recognize your current mindset. As you develop mindfulness, you can recognize and identify habituated thought patterns and then decide whether to use them or not. Mindfulness creates a distance between you and your thoughts, allowing you to see yourself separate from them. Incorporate mindfulness into your morning or evening routine and sit quietly for a few minutes (and practice gradually increasing the amount of time). When a thought comes to mind, turn your attention to your breathing instead of clinging to it.

2. Address Your Inner Critic

Your inner critic likes to convince you that it's not true, which often makes you feel pretty bad. Think of this voice as separate from you. Challenge the lie he is trying to feed you. Ask yourself. Is it true? Is there any evidence to support this claim? Another way is to thank this inner voice for their opinion and then say "no." I prefer not to fall into these negative thoughts. Alternatively, you may choose shorter, more direct answers, such as Not Now or Delete.

3. Know Your Triggers

It is essential to be aware of certain people, situations, and situations to trigger more negative thoughts. Meeting your boss or making important life decisions can make you overly critical of yourself or question your worth. Once you become aware of your triggers, you can better prepare to control your thoughts than go back to your old negative thinking patterns. It is also helpful to see which cognitive biases, such as those mentioned above, recur most often.

4. Write It Out

Writing down your feelings on paper is a great way to relieve your thoughts and learn more about them. We often don't realize how harmful our thoughts are. Negative thinking patterns become habitual over time and usually go unnoticed. Taking notes makes it easier to identify areas that need attention. You can also ask questions as soon as they appear in the article to ensure they are accurate and relevant. If not, let them go or replace them with more positive thoughts. Writing in a diary, the first thing you do when you wake up in the morning is the perfect time to write down your stream of consciousness on paper.

5. Recite A Mantra

Shouting out a mantra or positive affirmation is a great way to break free from your current negative thoughts. When you feel that something negative is coming, you can make it a habit to recite or focus on it several times throughout the day. You can choose words or phrases that remind you to focus on the present and focus more on the positive.

6. Change Your Surroundings

Sometimes the thoughts are so loud that it is best to change the physical environment. Go for a walk, run or meet friends in nature. The point is to engage in something other than a negative cycle so you can get back to the problem when you're in a cleaner space. Choose your favourite activity or place, and you will feel better. If you need to be with others, have people around you to encourage you to think positively. (Avoid the trigger!)

Negative stereotypes of thoughts are challenging to break, especially when habituated. Patterns that have existed for years don't disappear overnight, so it's essential to show compassion and patience for yourself as you work.

Chapter 22:

Five Smart Ways To Deal With Toxic People.

Who is toxic?

Toxic people are those who do things not good for our well-being. They are like a drop of poison in a 100-liter tank. We cannot dismiss it as harmless just because it is a single drop in 100 liters. It is still as harmful as is when alone. This analogy explains the effect of toxic people on your life. It does not matter if it is only one person or a whole group – they will still cause your downfall. Understanding toxic people for who they are will keep you safe from the untimely 'death' of your dreams and ambitions. It is not possible to avoid all toxic people because they too have their brighter side. The best you can do is to learn how to handle them. These are five smart ways to deal with toxic people:

1. Set Clear Boundaries

Boundaries are very important when dealing with toxic people. As a life principle, set boundaries with people you interact with because it is difficult at the beginning to distinguish between who is toxic and who is not. Even some non-toxic people could flip around mid-way. You never know. Clear boundaries will help people know when they are overstepping and they can retreat. For example, your associates should know better than not to talk ill of someone else in your presence. This seed of gossip they plant in you will make you one of them – a gossiper! Enforcement of boundaries set will keep you pure from many vices.

2. Stay Out Of Their Territory

There is this saying that if you do not want to trade with the Devil, stay out of His market. This is the same with toxic people. Do not follow them yet complain of their toxicity. You must choose one thing. Interact with people only when it is profitable and learn to leave when the agenda changes to toxicity. You cannot change them in their tuff. It is akin to a lone lion hunting in the territory of buffalos. Chances of success are slim.

3. Do Not Entertain Mediocrity

Before a trend takes root, it begins as a joke. This is how toxicity too begins to encroach. You see it as a small compromise that gradually grows and turns into something else. Being strict not to entertain mediocrity will save you a lot of trouble because people will know what to do or not when around you.

4. Constantly Review Your Working Plan

You need a daily reminder to keep you on your toes. Sometimes you do not even know that you have also been infected with the toxicity virus. You need to have a point of reference that will keep you in check. As you engage with different people, refer to the progress that you are making and whether anything is making you lag. This will help you quickly identify any toxic traits and deal with them before it goes out of hand. For example, can you identify at what point did the discussion change from how to help a friend to gossip behind his back on his failures?

5. Bring Other People Into The Picture

It will do good to involve someone else in your engagements who buys into your vision. They will help point out when you are losing it and when you are moving in the right direction. Let them be some kind of Prefect with no interest in whatever it is except to ensure you are not swallowed by your toxic partners. This is called the diluting effect. You dilute concentrated juice bought from supermarkets and do the same with some spirits too. You can employ this skill in how you handle toxic people.

Conclusion

Nobody is immune to a toxic environment. It is better to take preventive measures than wait to cure the problem when it is full-blown.

Chapter 23:

How To Stop Getting In Your Own Way

Are there valid reasons why you can't get things done? Absolutely. In fact, many times, external forces are working against you — think a sick child, flat tire, or global pandemic. There are, however, times when it turns out that we're our own biggest obstacle. We also call this self-sabotage. And, it can be brutal when it comes to productivity and our wellbeing. The good news? You can conquer this by getting out of your way. And, it's feasible by trying out the following techniques.

Remember Your Why

Instead of going through the motions and doing things for no reason, reconnect with your purpose. If you can't connect the dots between the activity and the big picture, then stop doing it. That doesn't mean avoiding tasks that you don't always enjoy. For example, as a new business owner, you might dread bookkeeping. However, it's an essential responsibility if you want your business to thrive. Remind yourself that maintaining your finances, sticking to a budget, and preparing your taxes can help you reach your business goals. And, as your business scales up, you can eventually hand this off to someone else.

Acknowledge Your Strengths

A strength is an activity that strengthens you. It doesn't have to be something that you excel at. Instead, it's something that you look forward to and "leaves you feeling energized. A strength is more appetite than ability, and it's that appetite that drives us to want to do it again; practice more; refine it to perfection. The appetite leads to the practice, which leads to performance. Leveraging your strengths and managing around your weaknesses isn't just about making yourself feel better. It's about conditioning yourself to contribute the best of yourself every day. It's about performance.

Nothing Compares To You — Except You

You bust your tail but aren't as productive as a colleague. You see that a friend just bought a new car or are enjoying a luxurious vacation. And, that just leaves you feeling like a failure. But, as Mark Twain once said, "comparison is the death of joy." Research backs that statement up. Comparing yourself to others leads to low self-confidence and depression. It can also make you green with envy, deplete motivation, and doesn't bring you closer to your goals. In short, if you measure yourself against others, you're always going to come short. Instead, practice gratitude. And, better yet, compare yourself by tracking your progress and celebrating what you've accomplished.

Run With The Right Crowd

Are you familiar with saying, "you are what you eat?" "Well, it's also true when it comes to who you keep company with. You may not realize this. But, the people you interact with on a daily basis directly influence who you are and what you do. Make sure you surround yourself with people who encourage you and hold you accountable—people from who you can learn positive habits from.

Remove Unnecessary Pressure

 Life is hectic enough. So, why make things worse by overcommitting or setting unrealistic expectations? Be realistic about what you can actually accomplish. If you don't have the availability or skillset, just say "no." For example, if you're calendar is already packed, decline time requests like unnecessary meetings or talking to a friend on the phone for two hours.

Engage In Self-Care

Some might consider self-care as a selfish act. In reality, it's making time for activities that leave you feeling calm and energized. These are vital in supporting your mental, physical, and emotional wellbeing. Examples can include going for a walk, journaling, hobbies, meditating, or taking a shower. Since time might appear to be a concern, add self-care to your calendar. For instance, you could leave an hour blank from 1 pm to 2 pm to spend however you like.

Avoid Ruminating

Ruminating is a cycle of repeating thoughts that you just can't shake. As a result, this can impair thinking and problem-solving. And, it can cause you to get stuck in your own head. To break free of these swirling thoughts, distract yourself. Examples are doing chores, reading, or calling a friend. You can also question your beliefs, set more attainable goals, and take small action steps to solve problems.

Chapter 24:

The Things That Matter

Today we're going to talk about a topic that I am very passionate about. Passionate because it has helped to guide each and every decision that I make on a daily basis. Having this constant reminder of the things that matter will put things in perspective for us - to eliminate the things that are taking up our time for the wrong reasons and to focus on the things that we actually want deep down in our hearts.

With that in mind, let's begin

How many of you can safely say that you know what truly matters in life? How do you define living a successful and fulfilling life? Is it by having a certain net worth? Is it by living a stress-free life? Is it seeing the world? Is it by serving a defined number of people? Is it by having 10 life-long friends that you can count on? Is it by having a certain number of kids? Or have you not really thought about what you really want out of life yet?

Before we can really gear our actions towards the direction that we want to lead it, we must first know exactly what those specific things we want to achieve are.

The things that matter in my life vary over time as I get older and wiser. When I was young, I used to think getting good grades, getting into a good university, and getting a good and stable job was all that really mattered, but I have soon come to realize that family, friends, and having people to hang out with were way more important than simply making money. There was a point in my life that I was so driven by money that I created a huge imbalance in my life by spending 99% of my time on my career. This lopsided drive caused me to neglect friendships, relationships, and soon people associated me with always being too busy for anything. I gradually stopped hanging out with anyone altogether. At first it was okay as I thought "hey, I finally have time to do whatever I want" and I don't have to be disturbed by meetups that would disrupt my workflow. But over time, I felt a gaping hole opening up somewhere deep inside that I could not seem to fill. I suddenly realized that I had successfully isolated myself from any and all relationships. This isolation felt increasingly lonely for me. I felt that I had no one to talk to when I was feeling down, no one to share my struggles with, no one to walk this journey with, and I knew I needed to do something about it. It was only after I started reconnecting with my friends did, I truly feel alive again. Having friends brought me more joy than money ever did or could. There's a saying that you can't buy happiness; the same is true for friendships - you can't buy them either. They have to be earned and built with trust and loyalty.

For those of you who are so career focused and money-minded, I share from experience that the destination may not be pretty if you do not have friends or family to share it with. Sure, you may afford a penthouse or a

Ferrari, but what does it really mean? Sure, you have a nice view and a fast ride, but can you share your life with it? When you are old and frail, can your house and car support you physically and emotionally? Don't make the same mistake I did for a good 3 years of my life. It was enough time for me to feel completely alone. No amount of acquiring things could fill that hole no matter how hard I tried. Sure, I had the fanciest Apple products, my iPad, iPhone, MacBook, iMac, AirPods, the list goes on. Sure, I could "make friends" with these shiny objects by using them everyday. But over time it just reminded me more and more that I had replaced people with gadgets, that I had replaced humans with Siri. It was really sad honestly.

Having friends that don't judge you or who don't care whether you have money or not, those are the real friends that you know you can count on. And I urge those of you who have neglected this big part to start reconnecting old friends or finding new ones altogether who share the same interests as you. Golf buddies, tennis buddies, karaoke buddies, these are good places to start searching for friends and getting the ice broken.

If starting a family is something that you really want in life, have you begun searching for a partner and planning how and when you expect that to happen for you? Sure, many of us think we may have a lot of time to do after we get our career going, but how many of us have heard stories of people who just never got off the bandwagon because they've become too busy with their careers? That maybe getting pregnant just never seems like the right time because you don't want to jeopardize your job. Or maybe that you never even got around to dating at all by the time you are 35 because you've become too busy being a general manager of your company. If having a career is the most important thing to you, then by all means go full steam ahead to achieve that goal. However, if family is something of great significance to you, you may want to consider starting that timeline right now instead of waiting. Remember the goal is to focus on the things that truly matter. If having a loving spouse who you can grow old with and having say 2 kids who can support you when you are old is what you really want, maybe waiting isn't such a good idea. Finding love takes practice. You will meet frogs along the way, and it takes time to grow a lasting relationship. Sure, you can rush a marriage if time is of the essence, but is that ideal? Personally, I believe a strong relationship takes 2-3 years to build. Do you have that type of runway to play with? Don't work yourself to death at your job only to find yourself rich and alone. Regret will come after for sure.

Whatever else you have defined as the things that matter to you, make sure that you never neglect those priorities. Sometimes life gets so busy and hectic that we forget to stop and refresh ourselves on what we really want to get out of life. It is all too easy for us to operate on autopilot - To set an alarm, go to work, gym, go home, take dinner, sleep, and repeat the day all over again. For weekends, we may be so exhausted from work that we just end up sleeping or wasting our weekend away only to begin the same routine again on Monday.

There's plenty of time for work decades down the road but dating relationships and friendships may not have that runway of time.

So, I challenge each and everyone of you to clearly define what the things that matter mean to you and to take consistent action in these areas day in and out until you can safely say you've already checked them off your bucket list.

Chapter 25:

How To Train Yourself to Be Optimistic and Positive

Positive thinking brings with it a whole host of benefits, such as better wellbeing and better sleep. To start reaping these benefits, check out how you can train your brain to be optimistic.

While many of us believe our happiness – or lack thereof – is based on external things, we're often the ones holding ourselves back. Many of us go through our days feeding ourselves negative messages we may not even be aware of, convincing ourselves we're "not good enough", "not clever enough" or "not attractive enough". To start thinking more positively, you need to change these messages. Try to look out for negative thoughts that pop into your head and replace them with positive messages. Write down some8 positive mantras and repeat them on a daily basis.

Most of us are happy to acknowledge other people's successes and accomplishments; however, when it comes to our own, we frequently play them down or ignore them entirely. To start thinking more positively about yourself, you need to regularly remind yourself of what you have – and can – achieve. Stop listening to your inner critic, reflect on your past achievements, and start to really appreciate your success and what you have to offer.

If you want to become an optimist, it can help to find yourself a positive role model. Whether it is a colleague, close friend or even a celebrity, think of the most unflappable, cheerful person you can. For the next few weeks, do an experiment and try to take a walk in their shoes. Whenever negativity starts creeping in or you find yourself in a difficult situation, think: "what would (insert name of chosen optimist) do?" Answer honestly, then try to follow suit.

It's important to remember that it isn't events themselves that make us unhappy, it is our interpretation and reaction to them, and while you can't always change events, you can change your response. When negative situations occur, try to reframe them by focusing on the positives or what you can learn from the situation. Maybe you have gained inner strength and resilience, grown closer to a friend through sharing your heartbreak or learned something about yourself. Try your best to focus on what you have learned and gained from your experience rather on than what you have lost.

When things don't go right in life, optimists tend to view each incident as an isolated event, while pessimists often look out for patterns of bad luck and think "if it happened once, it'll happen again". However, it is important not to try to predict the future based on what has happened before. Remember that a plan or relationship failing doesn't make you a failure and just because something disappointing has happened once (or more) it doesn't mean it will happen again.

What is gone is gone, and how you deal with the aftermath is the most important thing. There is no point apportioning blame, either on yourself or others. You have the power to change a situation and move on. It is so easy to say 'I should have done things differently' with the benefit of hindsight. However, if bad things have happened, look at tomorrow as exactly what it is — a new day — in which good things can happen, if you let them.

Chapter 26:

How Decluttering Brings You Happiness?

You must have heard people telling you about how decluttering benefited them in numerous ways. Some even exaggerate to say that it changed their lives entirely. But in today's fast world, everything is easy and quick - everything, but happiness. Happiness is not something we can just expect to have, but we can take steps to attain it as much as possible.

Today we're going to talk about how decluttering can help bring some of that happy state of mind into our lives. While it might sound tedious to think about decluttering your space, it has many wonderful benefits that can only be experienced once you begin the process.

Here are 7 Ways that decluttering can bring you happiness.

Keeping Your Stuff Organized Makes You Calm

If you say that a messy area is where you can feel more comfortable then most likely, you haven't experienced what a clean area can really do for you. It is human nature that we find peace in places and things that are organized and sorted. Take for example your bed - If you come back home to a made bed, you'll instantly feel relaxed seeing how your sheets and pillows are where they should be. But if they are strewn all over the place, you will find yourself in a fix.

In decluttering, you organize your stuff and place all your items where they should be. Each having a purpose and a place for being there. No excess, no extra items where they bring about a chaotic state of mind. Less is often more in this case. Consider packing up the excess stuff that takes up room on your desk, and either keep them in storage or consider placing them somewhere else where it does not interfere with the space that you are trying to keep organized.

I Found It! The Happiness Of Finding Something New

The Polaroid that slipped under your mattress and that pendant your mom gave you at the last family meet-up. Many such things are often lost in our rooms and homes - Items that you've either completely forgotten about, or items that you never even knew existed in the first place. Decluttering, by taking a methodical approach - cupboard by cupboard, shelf by shelf, and drawer by drawer, allows you to be extremely thorough. To the point where you might find hidden gems if the last time you did so was when you first moved into the house.

After all, what's better than finding your things that can potentially bring back memories? The joy you might feel is something that you should be excited about. Gifts, treasures, and even money could be on the list of items that you may find.

This Trip Down Memory Lane Brings Back Memories

This may sound poetic, but it is real. When you declutter and you go through your things piece by piece, you will inevitably come across loads of time capsule items such as your high school diary, pile of letters from past friendships that you saved when you were young, or even love letters from past admirers and past relationships. All of these things will bring you back in time when things were simpler, and you will experience the emotions as you go through all these relics once again as if you were receiving it for the first time.

You may even start to wonder what ever happened to those friends of the past – to wonder how they are doing right now, and to rekindle old friendships that time has stolen from us.

So many times, we don't even realize what we need, and maybe all we need is just a reminder you have had so many wonderful memories leading up to this day. Happy memories that help you realize that you will have many more wonderful memories ahead as well. Those events of happiness and warmth are lying in the corner of your room, waiting for you to open them.

There is nothing more essential than letting go of negativity

Who can agree that negativity is on the top of the list of the things we don't need in life? When you declutter and start sorting things out, you are also actively engaging in the process of sorting the negative energy too. You hold in the palm of your hands items that don't bring you joy, items that don't bring you happiness, and you make a conscious decision to put them aside or discard them away. At the same time you could be releasing anger, anxiety, sadness, and more from your space, leaving more room for happiness to flow in.

To Make Room For Space

To continue from the previous point, letting go of things that don't serve a purpose anymore will give you more freedom to enjoy the space you are working or living in. Decluttering does not mean that you can now acquire more things to fill up those gaps. Doing so defeats the purpose of clearing stuff out in the first place. Instead choose to leave your space empty unless something really compelling comes along that you simply cannot live without. What you may not realize is that having less things actually makes us feel happier than more.

Having more things means that we are never satisfied with how things are. It means having to spend more money to buy those things, working longer hours, and never really being at peace with just having enough stuff. We want to make room for the things that matter to us. Things that serve us rather become a slave to it. Choose your items wisely if you must, otherwise it is perfectly fine the way it is, clutter-free.

Getting rid of clutter can boost your productivity

A clear space equals a clear mind. Having a clean work desk or work environment serves as inspiration for us to create new and exciting things. When we see that pile of stuff in the corner, attention is always drawn away from us unexpectedly. This distraction shifts our focus from being productive into one of annoyance. Instead, consider placing only items that serve to motivate you and encourage you to chase your dreams. For example, either a motivational quote by a famous artist, photos of successful people you want to emulate, or even a vision board that you create for yourself. Things that create a deep and emotional reaction in you to make you want to be more productive. Chuck those ornaments and junk to one side and make room for these invaluable items.

To Invite More Positive Energy Into Your Space

When we learn to live with less things, we also subconsciously live in a state of abundance. Abundance in the sense that we disassociate having things with happiness. We untie ourselves from the notion that having more means increased happiness.

By only making room for the best things in our homes, we allocate our spending on one essential item that we designate to a specific area. For example, our couch or television. One that know we will love to use every single time we come home. We don't feel a need to buy another one just to fill up an empty space just because it is there. We buy one great desk and work chair to encourage us to be productive, and so on and so forth. Everything having a purpose and a place to be there.

Having more space also invites positivity because we allow ourselves the freedom to move around our house with ease. Not bumping into things, not having to maneuver in a weird fashion just to avoid a furniture. We flow freely from one room to the next. That is the ultimate goal that we should all try to achieve when we embark on the process of decluttering.

Conclusion

This world gives us a lot of things to maintain and live for and somewhere in this race, we forget that we are alive. This feeling of heartbreak and misery will never consume you if you keep taking care of yourself. Decluttering is an essential part of that act of looking after yourself. So invite more happiness into your life by decluttering… love yourself more and enjoy the sunlight of your life.

Chapter 27:

Remember The Feeling of Productivity

We all have a big list of ideas, that we want to work on. But we also tend to think that we miss a certain motivation to actually do something. But that is not true in most cases.

The true enemy of one's dreams is the lack of productivity or the feelings to remind you of staying productive like you once were.

Think about it! When you wake up, you pick up that phone, go through your notifications, and get stuck on something. Either consciously or unconsciously, something good or bad gets stuck in our mind, and now our whole day revolves around it.

This is a curse of the modern era. Technology has made us its slave and has taken a big chunk of our creative energies, efforts, and concentration.

Whenever you feel less motivated or have a tendency to get off-rails, remember your most recent productive moments. Try to recall the reasons and motives behind those actions that made you do something useful and productive.

People usually find their productive energies and wishes coming out in odd things. Like a cleaning fetish, some tendency to organize everything, always remaining ahead of everyone, never lose to anyone, or never skip a workout.

Skepticism isn't always bad or worry-some, not unless you lack a sense of purpose for being skeptical. And this feeling of not being able to get yourself to focus on better things is the flaw leading to failure. It's not the lack of motivation or effort, rather the usage of your energies elseware.

We often procrastinate either unintentionally or habitually and end up doing trivial activities that don't help us much. Instead, they shape up your routine in a constant cycle of unsuccessful events.

To remove all your distractions. Put away your phone, your laptop, your iPad. Anything that might attract you into spending one more minute and I'll get started.

If you can't give up these things, that's fine. Let's make a game out of it.

For one week, make a deal with yourself. Write three goals for each day and start making effort for them. Force yourself to not touch your phone till you get at least one of the things done. As soon as you get something done, now, you are allowed to have a bit of distraction to regain some thoughts and perspective.

It's never about perfection, it's always about progress. If you can hold yourself for a little time, with practice you will enter a stage of mind, where you are not reliant on anything but yourself.

Productivity isn't just a set of acts that you perform in a block of time. Productivity is the meaning that we attach to things. Productivity is the mindset that drives your life around a path. Productivity is a choice.

But this feeling of productivity isn't a public garden, rather a hard bet that requires you to make a gutsy call of hardship and stamina.

So, get out of your head, Stop thinking about what you need to do, and start doing it.

Chapter 28:

Affirmations For Men

It is true that things have a course of action, and that everything has a cycle. This is true for every one of us. We all grow, and we all prevail. Sometimes we all get distracted and reach a point where don't want to take it anymore and just want to be left alone.

We have lived long enough to come to terms with the way things are and the rituals of the world. We should be able to appreciate things as they stand right now. We should be able to look for the good in everything in and around us.

It does get hard more than often, and we just want things to get a bit easier, but they never really do. The fog of self-doubt and constant failure make it hard to look for the bright edges, but here is when the positive affirmations play a vital role.

Affirmations are the things you say and do to make yourself feel more alive and remind yourself that you have more in your life than you think you don't.

We all have these small quotes or commands that we give to ourselves for the sake of growing in every hard time. We tell ourselves that we have to stand form in these rough times and one day we will grow tall and above all these swamps of uncertainty.

We men have a lot on our plate, and we go through a ton of grind in our everyday life. It is easy to lose sight of our habits and our passions when we are presented with a barrage of hardships. But never can we afford to get washed away will all the beating in the world. Because we are strong beings, and we need to stay strong for not only us but also the people that depend on us.

How To Create Your Own Positive Affirmations?

So how do create these feelings of self-motivation, these quotations of deep dedication, these positive affirmations?

What do you need for an affirmation to have an impact?

I have created four clear criteria for each affirmation to meet.

l The first one, obviously your affirmation should be optimistic.
l Secondly, whatever you create, it should be in the present.
l Your affirmations should be specific to a particular problem or a particular goal.

l Lastly but most importantly, all your affirmations should be related to yourself.

The best affirmations that you can create are the ones that are derived from a negative habit or ritual. But how change things around?
How can you take something negative and change it into a positive statement to make you grow?

How can you make these positive affirmations? Or if you have some already, how can you make them work for them?

Let's start it the other way around. Let's say you think that you are not good at your job. You think that you are not being as successful as others. You think that you are not worthy of success. You need to let go off of these thoughts. The longer you hold on to them, the more you will drown in the sorrow and the less capable you will be to get the position you always dreamed of.

Stop thinking: "I am not performing well. I cannot be the employ of the month. I am not getting the raise this year". Instead, start thinking: "I am a competitive employee. I can get the job done before time. I will get all the bonuses this year."

The minute you start to think positive, you will feel a surge of completeness and wholesomeness.

Let me help you craft some positive affirmations for yourself.

Let's start with a general and most basic one,

"From this day onwards, I am going to bid farewell to every bad memory and every regret. I have nothing to be ashamed of as I am only a human."

You are trapped inside a body that is smart but has its restrictions. We all make mistakes and this is what makes us mortal.

You cannot live a life of fear and regret. You cannot possibly be charged with punishment for every little mistake that you make consciously or unconsciously.

"I am Strong and resilient and I can make my own choices. No one can control me by their opinions about me or others."

"I am confident about my body and its true limits. I can push my limits to where ever I want them to be."

"I am valued by my loved ones, and they can help me be a better version of myself."

"My feelings and my emotions are as important as anyone else's. I have a right to be heard and I will always raise my voice for the right cause."

"I am worthy of Mental and Monetary stability and peace."

Can I create my own Meditation Mantra?

"I deserve more for my efforts and I deserve appraisal and success for my hard work."

"I am an emotional being and no one can judge my manliness on this. I have all rights to share my feelings and tears if I am feeling down."

"My strength is my ideas and I have some great ones. I can express my concerns with full responsibility as I have my experiences and knowledge to back them."

"No one can reach my inner core and change it. Neither will I let anyone do that."

"I deserve to be happy and I deserve the abundance in life that I have longed for."

"I can achieve any goal in life and no one can tear me down till I remain strong and keep my intentions neat."

"What I have lost is what was meant to go, but what I want is meant to be mine."

"Some challenges I can take head-on. The ones I shouldn't engage in, I know when to walk away from those."

"I can make new friends, I just need to believe in people."

"I can walk away from toxic friends, I just need to gather some courage and speak out my heart."

"People will get impressed once they get to know me better. I can prove to be a great friend for anyone who wants my company."

"Good things will happen for me if I stay loyal to my cause and I will not let anyone stand in my way."

"I am a magnet to new opportunities and I am ready to do everything new and scary that looks me in the eye today."

"I can be resilient and I am resilient. I always learn from my mistakes and I keep moving forward."

"I define my purpose and that purpose is carved within. No one sketches my purpose and my path for me."

"I say what I deem right and what I say is right. No fluff and no bluff."

"Bad things will always happen, but I will always be able to make the best out of every bad situation."

"I am a proud being with a lot to look back on and a lot to look up to."

"I don't need anyone to stand up for me or to justify my decisions. My actions and their consequences will answer for themselves."

"I am not perfect but I can try to be the best I can be."

"My worth is not what others think of me. My worth is the people that depend on me and the ones that look up to me."

"I am more than capable of achieving greatness as long as I stick to my basic goals and the rest will be history."

"I don't have space for humility in my life. I am proud and content with whatever I have right now."

Remember the Fundamentals

"I don't need anyone else to measure my greatness and my abilities."

"No one is more resourceful than me and I am the greatest asset anyone can have."

"I have to create my own calm and get rid of all my untroubled past."

"I am a good father, a good brother, a good partner, and a good friend."

"I am the bravest person I know. No one can declare me a coward and a quitter."

"My spirits are on their highest every day I wake up."

"I am thankful for everything I have done today and I have am more grateful for what I shall do better tomorrow."

"No goal is small and I am determined to fulfill all my legitimate desires no matter what cost I have to pay for them."

"My life has all the meaning in it already, I just have to look around all the corners."

"I should start every day with a positive feeling and end every day with a better one."

"I cannot change anyone or their perceptions about me but I can change my response towards them."

"I don't need anyone to boost my confidence. I am the biggest cause and source of my inspirations."

"Happiness is not a choice, it is my obligation towards myself and others."

"My efforts and my intentions will eventually pay off, no matter how hard the world tries to turn me down."

"No one can judge me on my looks or my age. My history has worth no matter how short or long it is."

"I am a learner, and I will always be a work in progress. I don't expect me to be perfect."

"I have great respect for my body and everything in it. The things I can do with it are the blessing for which I can never be grateful enough."

"I can compete with any coworker at any level, but no one can tell me when to."

"Whoever needs my help shall find me standing and fighting beside them at every rough corner."

"I have left all my baggage behind and I won't have any to drag me down ever again."

"My workout sessions will keep my mind and my body engaged for the greater good of a long and healthy life."

"I fulfill all my duties and I deserve all the love and respect in return."

"My smile is enough to keep my sorrows away and it will someday be a source of light for someone else in need of happiness."

"I need to learn to say 'No' without needing to explain myself. The best weight I can lose is the weight of other people's opinion of me."

Words are just words and if you don't put them to good use. Life is a rough ride. A little more for some and a little smooth for the others. But the jitters are all the same for everyone.

You can have a good functioning life even if you don't have something to look out for in life. But the purpose of life is not fulfilled if you learn the process.

Life was never meant to be lived like a script written by a robot. Life has a lot of things that are dynamic and a little more complicated than sleeping, getting up, eating, working on a timetable, eating again, and finally back to sleep.

We need to create more things in life where we have a lot more to live for and new ways to cherish life. We need to find meaning in every aspect of life. We need to find productive relationships and productive hobbies. We need to defend our rights and our actions. We need to open up about our emotions and our struggles. We need appreciation and we all need the warmth of humanly touch. But what we can't do is to keep a distance from everyone that loves us or everyone that wants to pin us down.

Keep reminding yourself of these affirmations every day and you won't have a day in your life when you don't feel a spark that keeps you going in life.

We have a duty towards ourselves to make the best out of everything in life till the time we finally close our eyes and say our goodbyes to this world!

Chapter 29:

Affirmations for Women

Ecstasy and melancholy are a part of human nature if you follow Shakespeare's view who places joys and sorrows beside each other. These emotions affect the way we perform our daily routine tasks or the way we interact with one another. Exuberance, However, levitates our mood and keeps us motivated to give a new start or to accomplish the pending tasks. On the other hand, If gloominess prevails, How are we going to get on with our lives?

What If A Tiring Attitude Prevails?

How are you going to come out of this dismal zone and work with new energy? It's because you cannot justify your claim to your boss by saying that "My apologies for being careless sir, I could not meet the deadline because I was in a bad mood yesterday!".

What I believe is that a person cannot be inculcated with the same thrilling behavior or the energy they had the first day when they joined the company. Or when they started to chase the required goal. Your energy starts decaying and you need someone to stimulate you to get back on track.

Well, that role of induction is played by your Affirmations. Affirmations are such positive statements that persuade you to get back on your horses. You read those motivating statements and after absorbing the vibe, you feel like flying with high spirits and that is the only thing you need in life when things are not going well.

Do Women Rely On Emotions?

Women are agile and energetic at one time and truly dependable on their emotions at the same time. But you cannot say that being emotional is what makes someone fragile. To elaborate something through sentiments is rather a beautiful art of expression.

A woman has the whole responsibility to nurture her child. However, this era of Modernity doesn't confine a woman to merely a household unit. Rather women are working alongside men.

It is quite Natural that handling the workload along with daily chores creates a hectic routine with which a person often gets fed up. At that point, you need someone to prompt you up in such a way that you feel better about your existence.

Do you feel like you can do it?

Your affirmations will play a significant role in this regard.

Here, let me help you boost your energy by stating some. That might prove to be beneficial for you in the future.

Does Your Mental Peace Make Any Difference?

You are struggling with your daily routine schedule, and you don't have time for yourself. No doubt, you are a person always up with the lark. No matter, how much money you're making, it can't be worth it if it is costing you your peace, so tell yourself:

"I prefer my mental peace over everything as all of those storms meddling into my peace are not worth considering "

You are an independent person with a free soul …what I bring back to my mind is:

"I don't rely on anyone for my happiness. My happiness revolves around my soul."

It is normal if you are not feeling that energy lately that you used to feel when you started your job or work. I know it happens sometimes when you are down, and you need some motivation in your life. You just get up in the morning to make a living. You feel like things are not interesting anymore.

You are just surviving the day. Well, That's not a big deal. First let me remind you that we, humans need constant motivation in our lives as we are not consistent in our aims. Remind yourself that:

"I am a competent woman with an invincible Mindset. I am a woman with countless shortcomings and I admire myself with my defects due to which I stand out from others."

Why Do We Need Acknowledgment?

Acknowledgment of your abilities will elevate your confidence,

"My exceptional skills elevate my morale to move ahead I respect my people who encourage me to strive till the end. So, I am not afraid of challenges in my life. I accept them rather, and surpass them transcendently."

"The acceptance of my flaws reflects the real me. And I adore the real me"

"I embrace my errors and make little effort to improve myself. However, I never let anything shake my confidence."

How Do You Define Your Success?

You are the one deciding your future. Your success or failure is not defined by society.

"I have the vision to pursue in my life and I am ready to chase it."

I see people falling into agony or wretchedness just because they meet failure. You need to make yourself clear that a particular circumstance does not mark your aptitude or your potential.

"Being a woman is the real thing to brag over. What I enjoy even more is being a successful woman."

You don't meet failure until you decide to count it as destruction for yourself.

"I am a woman of unstoppable energy. I grab the opportunities and spend my energies on them."

You can stand out. Create some noise in reticence and keep on trying until you achieve what you aim for…. Just like I keep on evoking myself that:

"I choose career above all. Rest can wait!!! I have erased all of the self doubts that were once hindrances in my way of success."

Your Relations Strengthen Your Expertise

It's okay if you cannot deal with the situations right now. It's okay If you are just in a perplexed state of mind, not absorbing things quite well.

We all go through such a phase in our lives where we have to understand our relations but we are stuck in that constant dilemma of How should we deal with it?

Prompt yourself just like I did when I went through this phase where I was afraid of losing the purity of my relations that I once struggled hard to maintain.

"I appreciate all relationships of mine because they are the ones who are bearing me even when I don't want to live anymore. I deserve to be around those people who love me and motivate me to fight the upcoming obstacles."

Sometimes, relations for which you show concern need your approval or appreciation too. It's because people who love you, support you no matter how hard the circumstances get.

"Your words are just ornaments. Your vibe is what attracts me. My mind is truly occupied with you and I can't get over it."

Your significant ones fight back for you till the end. So it's necessary to adore your bond with Them. And I feel it's not hard to say that;

"You are the reason I cherish every day."

We often get off our track and need someone to drive us back. So appreciate your relations to conquer serenity;

"My family and friends are the ones who support me out in my tough times."

You deserve to enjoy all the care and affection from your people.

Is Self-Love Important?

It's true, that this world continues to drag you down by tormenting you that you are not pretty, You are not a worthy woman, you don't deserve love and respect from this society. This society would not give you the privilege you desire for. And to be honest, This is what our community does. They intimidate you to the point where you think of yourself as an inferior bug in society. And how can you expect to give love to your relations when you don't love yourself. It's quite ridiculous that we don't put ourselves in the first place, We don't love ourselves and we strive to make other people feel special with our existence. What I mean to say is that:

"Self-love is the element we need to implant in ourselves."

Do you know what is the key to self-admiration? It's **Forgiveness**. Well, It might seem to be a trivial point to you. So let me elaborate you the other way round. When you don't forgive others, when you don't let the things go from your heart, It just keeps on storing there creating a whole bunch of mess in your heart. You start to feel toxic about everything including you, your friends, your family, and This world appears to be a suffocating globe and I am sure you would detest living such a life. So, say this to yourself:

"Starting from today, I am going to forgive others for my own mental peace."

The day you stop feeling hatred and malice towards others, will be the day you're about to love yourself.

Can Money Make You Content?

The endeavor for making money will remain until humans continue to exist. We cannot negate the fact that money is important for today's survival, as it is an inevitable need. To say that It should not be the priority is just being a childish act. You are putting yourself in a state of oblivion.

However, you need to understand this point that to make money to survive is important but to line up yourself in the devouring race to compile wealth, not considering your health and mental peace is something that will put you in a brewing situation. You can secure your mental peace by Following these simple steps:

1. First of all, Know your worth. You don't deserve agitation and distress just to make money in the end. Give it a thought, you are striving for a decent life. You have that money in abundance, but you are not satisfied.

You have that persistent stress in your mind that refrains you from living life, worth satisfactory.

"I know my Worth and I don't allow anyone to question it."

2. After realizing your worth, eliminate all the negative perceptions and self-doubts out of your mind and assert yourself that:

"I have deleted all the negative thoughts that had kept me from attaining my goals in the past. I have distanced myself from toxicity and my sole aim is to inhale positivity rather than instilling negativity".

3. Eradicate your past regrets and don't feel remorse about what happened in your back days. Each day brings opportunities for you to upgrade yourself. Resentment is too heavy to hold so remove the remorseful emotions that are perturbing you and replace them with healthy emotions:

"I do not hold a grudge for my past actions. I just focus on being a better person in the future and that's what matters. I want a life inculcated with an expression of jubilation."

Miracles do happen when you explore yourself and your potentials to achieve wonders. So instead of keeping grudges in hearts and accumulating toxicity in yourself, let those feelings go.

"I don't hold regrets about anything. I just focus on what keeps me happy."

4. Imbue Positive thoughts in your mind

"No one can turn me down except my thoughts. So, I plan on feeding positive thoughts to my mind. I feel that better days are waiting for me. I just need to believe in the process."

You need to focus on the present moment and make it worth living. Life would be much more easier and meaningful to you in this way. People who don't permit the depressed part of their lives to affect the present moments are the ones who have got the key to live a peaceful life.

To sum it all up, I am insisting you adopt these attributes in your life. These are some of the essential affirmations that I have enlisted promoting Inner peace, self-love, confidence, Relationships' significance, and many more. I feel that you should apply these positive assertions in your life to shatter the upcoming obstacles in your way and make your life much more ambitious and effective.

Always remember, you are smart, you are worthy and above all, you are enough. The day you lose your confidence is the day you lose everything. Make a commitment to yourself that, I will never let anyone take my smile from me, everything will become more and more achievable and bearable.

Chapter 30:

Stop Hitting That Snooze Button

Life is about the things you can take control of. You live your life day by day. So, every day in your life is a small part that starts with you waking up and ends with you going back to bed. You sleep every night after setting up at least five different alarms. Why do you set all these alarms and then sleep until the last? It is simple; You set these alarms because there have been tasks on your mind that you must do.

You set more than one alarm because you know you will snooze them all for sure. You can't get up on the first alarm because you are too lazy and you don't have any discipline in your life. Your alarm keeps buzzing, and you wait till the last ring to either snooze it or for it to end. But this is your deciding moment. This is your time to decide if you want to get up or keep snoozing as you have been avoiding and snoozing opportunities your whole life.

This is a battle with yourself to test if you will hit the snooze or if you will get up and do what is necessary. You set alarms to help you get up when the natural causes are not enough. You might be a deep sleeper or a light sleeper, but you need some aid or reminder to get up in the morning. But when you hit that snooze button, you have essentially broken the determination with which you set that alarm last night.

Maybe this was your last chance to succeed. Perhaps this was your last chance to get out of this state of depression and laziness. You aren't probably the guy who promotes success on one's own actions. You can't even handle an alarm on your phone; how do you plan to take the world's mockery when you fail at other things in your life.

If you train yourself to be subconsciously active even before you hear the first alarm, this means you are well equipped to break your sleep cycles whenever you want. This mirrors your dedication to your work and your control over your own body.

If you don't hit the snooze button and go out to work, it will not matter too much if you fail out there. Why? Because now you started your day with success when you acted against your wishes to sleep a little longer and didn't hit that snooze button. Now you are on a power curve, and you feel good about the following things because now you are hopeful. Because now you know you can bring a change within yourself.

When you didn't hit that snooze button, you showed yourself how much this day means to you and how much of a promising character you are. Life is long enough to hit the snooze some other time, but for now, you need to seize the day as it might never be like this again.

www.ingramcontent.com/pod-product-compliance
Lightning Source LLC
Chambersburg PA
CBHW072059110526
44590CB00018B/3245